LAUGH OUT LOUD!

THE ANIMAL ANTICS
JOKE BOOK

Sean Connolly and Kay Barnham

WINDMILL
BOOKS

New York

Published in 2012 by Windmill Books, LLC
303 Park Avenue South, Suite # 1280, New York, NY 10010-3657

First Edition

Editor: Joe Harris
Illustrations: Adam Clay
Layout Design: Notion Design

Library of Congress Cataloging-in-Publication Data

Connolly, Sean, 1956–
  The animal antics joke book / by Sean Connolly and Kay Barnham. — 1st ed.
     p. cm. — (Laugh out loud!)
  Includes index.
  ISBN 978-1-61533-362-2 (library binding) — ISBN 978-1-61533-400-1 (pbk.) — ISBN 978-1-61533-464-3
  (6-pack)
  1. Animals—Juvenile humor. 1. Barnham, Kay. II. Title.
  PN6231.A5C66 2012
  818'.602—dc22
                                    2010052137

Printed in China

For more great fiction and nonfiction, go to www.windmillbooks.com

CPSIA Compliance Information: Batch #AS2011WM: For Further Information contact Windmill Books, New York, New York at 1-866-478-0556
SL001836US

CONTENTS

Why are dogs such bad dancers?
They have two left feet.

What's worse than raining cats and dogs?
Hailing taxis.

What happened to the cat that swallowed a ball of wool?
She had mittens.

How can you keep a wet dog from smelling?
Hold its nose.

Have you put some more water in the goldfish bowl?
No. It still hasn't drunk the water I put in when I first bought it!

ANIMAL ANTICS

Hey, you can't fish here, this is a private lake!
I'm not fishing, I'm teaching my pet worm to swim!

How do fleas get from one animal to another?
They itch hike!

What's the special offer at the pet store this week?
Buy one cat—get one flea!

What do you call a multistory pigpen?
A styscraper.

Why did the dog wear
gloves?
Because it was a boxer.

ANIMAL ANTICS

My dog's a blacksmith.
How can you tell?
When I tell him off, he makes a bolt for the door.

Why did it take the Dalmatian so long to choose a vacation?
He was looking for just the right spot.

Why was the cat scared of the tree?
Because of its bark.

What animal wears a long coat in the winter and pants in the summer?
A dog!

What is a good pet for small children?
A rattlesnake!

What type of dog can tell the time?
A watchdog.

How do you spell mouse trap using only 3 letters?
C A T!

Which pets are the noisiest?
Trumpets!

What did the dog say when it sat on some sandpaper?
Ruff!

Classified ad in local paper:
"Dog free to good home—eats anything. Loves children!"

How do you stop a dog from barking in the back seat of a car?
Put it in the front seat.

What are dog biscuits made from?
Collie-flour!

Johnny: Mom, is our dog metric?
Mom: Why do you ask?
Johnny: Because Dad said it has just had a liter of puppies!

Why did the dog limp into the Wild West saloon?
He came to find the cowboy who shot his paw!

ANIMAL ANTICS

I think I'm turning into a young cat.
You must be kitten me!

What do you call a cat that chases outlaws?
A posse cat!

What do you get if you cross an insect and a rabbit?
Bugs Bunny.

Did you hear about the well-behaved cat?
It was purrfect.

One boy says to another boy, "My pet's called Tiny."
"Why?" asks his friend.
"Because he's my newt."

ANIMAL ANTICS

Knock, knock!
Who's there?
Alf.
Alf who?
Alf feed the cat while you're on vacation!

What do cats drink in the desert?
Evaporated milk.

What do you call a column topped with a statue of a famous cat?
A caterpillar!

What do you call a cat with eight legs?
An octopus.

What do you call a woman with a cat on her head?
Kitty.

What did the dog say when his owner stopped him from chewing the newspaper?
"You took the words out of my mouth!"

What do you get if you drop birdseed in your shoes?
Pigeon toes.

What did the clean dog say to the dirty dog?
Long time no flea!

My dog is a real problem. He chases anything and everything on a bike. I don't know what to do.
Just take his bike away!

Which cats are great at bowling?
Alley cats.

What sort of dog is good at looking after children?
A baby setter.

Doctor, I think I'm a cat!
How long have you felt like this?
Since I was a kitten!

What do you get if a cat sits on a beach at Christmas?
Sandy claws!

First cat: Where do fleas go in the winter?
Second cat: Search me!

What happened to the Scottish cat that ran into the road without looking?

It was kilt!

How do you find a lost dog?

Make a sound like a bone!

Teacher: Can you define "dogmatic?"

Pupil: Is it a robot pet?

Did you hear about the cat that sucked a lemon?

He was a sourpuss.

What's a horse's favorite sport?

Stable tennis.

ANIMAL ANTICS

What's the difference between a well-dressed gentleman and an exhausted dog?
One wears an expensive suit and the other just pants.

Doctor, I feel as sick as a dog.
I'll make an appointment for you to see a vet!

Mom: Did you put the cat out?
Kid: I didn't need to. It wasn't on fire!

What do you use to clean a cat's hair?
A catacomb.

What do you give
a sick parakeet?
Tweetment!

Why was the pig covered in ink?
Because it lived in a pen.

Why do pigs make terrible drivers?
They're all road hogs.

How do you make a cat happy?
Send it to the Canary Islands!

What do you call the place where cats and dogs go to get new tails?
A retailer!

What do you call a dog that is always rushing around?
A dash-hound!

ANiMAL ANTiCS

Where do you buy baby birds?
At the chickout.

What do you get if you leave a parrot cage open?
A polygon.

What do you get if you cross a honeydew and a sheepdog?
A melon collie.

Doctor, I think I'm a dog.
Well, take a seat and I'll have a look at you.
I can't—I'm not allowed on the furniture!

Did you hear about the boy who spilled spot remover on his dog?
The dog vanished.

Why did the chicken sit on an ax?
She wanted to hatchet.

What did the traffic officer put on the car outside the dog kennel?
A barking ticket.

What's a dog's favorite hobby?
Collecting fleas.

What does your pet snake become if he gets a government job?
A civil serpent!

Why did the cat say "woof?"
It was learning a foreign language.

What do you get when you cross a parrot and a cat?
A carrot!

ANIMAL ANTICS

Where do huskies train for dogsled races?
In the mushroom.

Why did the dogs jump in the lake?
To catch a catfish.

What type of pet just lies around doing nothing?
A carpet.

Why did the dog chase his own tail?
He was trying to make ends meet.

Which dog wears a white coat and looks through microscopes?
A lab!

What do you call a prisoner's parakeet?
A jail bird!

ANIMAL ANTICS

Why did the cat pounce on the computer?
Because he saw a mouse.

What's happening when you hear "Meow—splat! Woof—splat!"
It's raining cats and dogs.

What has more lives than a cat?
A frog—it croaks every night.

Did you hear about the cat who drank three saucers of water in one go?
She wanted to set a new lap record!

Doctor, I feel like a dog!
Sit!

Why do dogs wag their tails?
Because no one else will do it for them.

**What's red
and green and
jumps out of planes?**
A parrot-trooper!

Why did the Dalmatian go to the eye doctor?
He was seeing spots.

What did Shakespeare's cat say?
"Tabby or not tabby..."

Why do dogs run in circles?
Because it's hard to run in squares.

What do you get when you cross a dog with a sheep?
A sheep that can round itself up.

What did the cowboy say when the bear ate his hunting hound?
Doggone!

What do parakeets wear to the beach?
Beakinis.

What happens when cats fight?
They hiss and make up.

What do you call rabbits marching backward?
A receding hare-line.

ANIMAL ANTICS

Why do terriers make great fighter pilots?
Because they're good in a dogfight.

Why did the girl oil her pet mouse?
Because it squeaked.

What did the bunny say to the carrot?
It's been nice gnawing you.

What do you use to comb a rabbit?
A hare-brush.

What's more astounding than a talking dog?
A spelling bee.

22

ANIMAL ANTICS

What do you say to a dog
before he eats?
"Bone appetite!"

What do you call a cat
that does tricks?
A magic kit.

What do you call a dog
in jeans and a sweater?
A plain-clothes police
dog.

What did the canary say when its new cage fell apart?
"Cheep! Cheep!"

What do you call a guard dog with a cold?
A germy shepherd.

How does a cat sing the musical scale?
Do-re-meow.

What do you call a hamster that can pick up an elephant?
Sir!

What does a cat say when he gets hurt?
Mee-OW!

How did the puppy stop the DVD player?
He used paws.

What do you get when you cross a dog with an elephant?
A really nervous mailman.

ANIMAL ANTICS

Why are dogs longer at night than during the day?
Because they are let out in the evening and taken in in the morning.

What happens if you mix a bird, a car, and a dog?
A flying carpet.

What kind of cat keeps the grass short?
A lawn meower.

Cat bumper sticker:
"Life is hard—then you nap."

What kind of bird does construction work?
A crane.

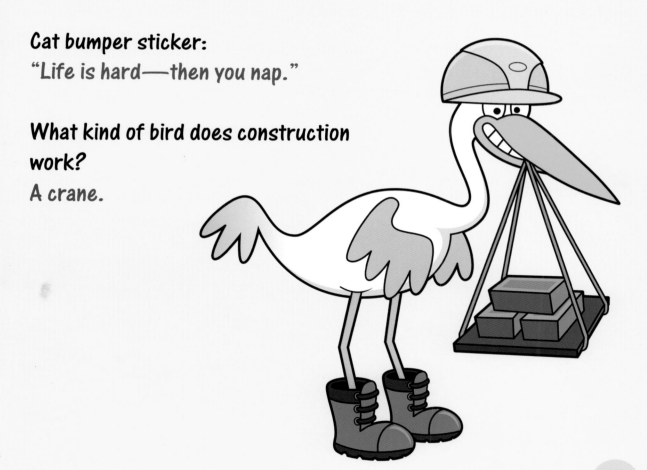

ANIMAL ANTICS

Did you hear about the pig who walked around the world?
He was a globetrotter.

Why is it called a "litter" of puppies?
Because they mess up the whole house.

What happened when the dog went to the flea circus?
He stole the show!

What did one flea say to the other flea?
"Should we walk or take the dog?"

Which birds steal from the bathtub?
Robber ducks.

What do you get when you cross a parrot with a pig?
An animal that hogs the conversation.

What do cats use to make coffee?
A purr-colator.

Which cat led the Chinese revolution?
Chairman Meow.

What do lazy dogs do for fun?
They chase parked cars.

ANIMAL ANTICS

Why did the turtle
cross the road?
To get to the
Shell station.

Why do birds
lay eggs?
Because if
they dropped
them, they'd
break.

What do you call a
parakeet that joins the Ice Capades?
A cheep skate.

Where do young dogs sleep when they camp out?
In pup tents.

What do you call a veterinarian with laryngitis?
A hoarse doctor.

ANiMAL ANTiCS

When is it unlucky to see a white cat?
When you're a mouse.

Why don't you need a license for a cat?
Because cats can't drive!

What do you give a pony with a sore throat?
Cough stirrup.

Who always succeeds?
A parakeet with no teeth.

Why was the toucan kicked out of the hotel?
Because he had an enormous bill!

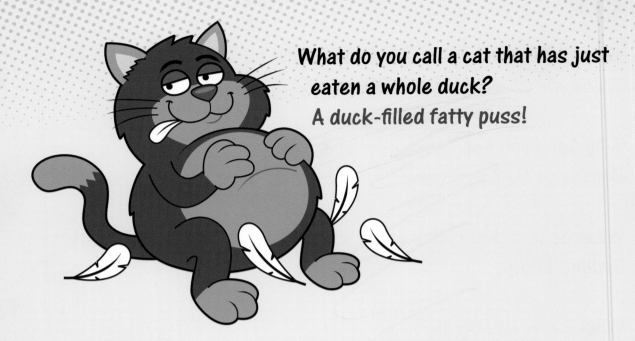

What do you call a cat that has just eaten a whole duck?
A duck-filled fatty puss!

Teacher: Some plant names begin with the word "dog." Think of dogwood and dog rose. Can anyone think of another beginning with dog?
Pupil: Collie-flower!

Why did the teen pig have to tidy her room?
Her mom said it looked like a pigsty.

Can a cat play patty-cake?
Paw-sibly.

What's it called when a dog does a TV commercial?
Ad-fur-tisement.

What do you call a Scottish parrot?
A macaw!

Which breed of dog can jump higher than a tree?
Any breed—trees can't jump!

What do you get if you cross a dog with a cheetah?
A dog that chases cars—and catches them!

In which month do dogs bark the least?
In February—it's the shortest month!

How did the little Scottish dog feel when he saw the monster?
Terrier-fied.

Glossary

blacksmith (BLAK-smith) someone who makes and repairs metal objects

catacomb (KA-tuh-kohm) an underground place where dead bodies are buried

dogmatic (dawg-MA-tik) stubborn about your ideas

evaporate (ih-VA-puh-rayt) to turn a liquid to vapor, especially when it is heated

saloon (suh-LOON) a place where people in the Wild West bought alcoholic drinks

Further Reading

Chatterton, Martin. *What a Hoot!* New York: Kingfisher, 2005.

Dahl, Michael. *Roaring with Laughter*. Mankato, MN: Picture Window Books, 2004.

Winter, Judy A. *Jokes About Animals*. Mankato, MN: Capstone Press, 2010.

Index

Web Sites

For Web resources related to the subject of this book, go to: www.windmillbooks.com/weblinks and select this book's title.